PERFEKT CRIME

A Comedy
by

DAVID TRISTRAM

A Flying Ducks Publication

INSPECTOR DRAKE & THE
PERFEKT CRIME

Casting

Inspector Drake and the Perfekt Crime requires five actors - three male, two female. The characters, in order of appearance, are:

Sergeant Plod
Doctor Short
Inspector Drake
Sabrina
Miss Short

Set Design

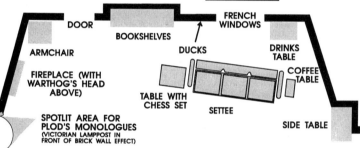

DOOR

BOOKSHELVES

FRENCH WINDOWS

DUCKS

DRINKS TABLE

ARMCHAIR

COFFEE TABLE

FIREPLACE (WITH WARTHOG'S HEAD ABOVE)

TABLE WITH CHESS SET

SETTEE

SPOTLIT AREA FOR PLOD'S MONOLOGUES
(VICTORIAN LAMPPOST IN FRONT OF BRICK WALL EFFECT)

SIDE TABLE

Drake's Entrance

The script calls for Inspector Drake to make a rather unusual entrance - up through the middle cushion of the settee. In the original production, this was achieved by a combination of a specially doctored settee, and a fortuitously placed trap door. Not everyone, of course, will be able to rely on either of these devices. Not to worry. Though the effect is a great hit with audiences and well worth trying for if you can manage it, Drake can, if all else fails, quite simply pop up from behind the settee. If you opt for this simple solution, you'll have to slightly adapt the ending, as follows.

Instead of Drake disappearing back down the settee the way he came, he approaches Miss Short behind the settee and closes in for a kiss. Just before impact, Sergeant Plod pops up between them - interrupting as he has down throughout the play - and merely says "Can I have a word, sir?" (Lights, Curtain)

For this option, just make sure that the settee is sufficiently far back to cover the sightlines to the french windows, so that Plod can crawl back on and hide behind the settee after exiting through the door.

Lighting

There are, essentially, just four lighting states. Full stage lights, blackout, a spotlight for Plod's narrative monologues, and a central spotlight.

Your lighting designer may, of course, wish to elaborate beyond these, depending on the resources available, but start with the basics and aim for razor-sharp timing.

Music

The use of well chosen and well executed music can greatly enhance the effect of any production - and this is especially true of Inspector Drake & The Perfekt Crime. It's recognized, though, that not every society has access to good, reliable sound systems, reel-to-reel tape machines, and the like.

The script makes mention of various points where a short musical link or dramatic stab would be appropriate but, like most things, they are not essential. It's far better to stay well within your technical limitations than to risk embarrassment or bad timing with music, so if in doubt, leave it out.

You could even consider a novel alternative to some of the music stabs, such as the actors, or back-stage staff, singing the stab live (badly). If you can get away with it anywhere, you can get away with it in this play, and it may prove even funnier than a slick pre-recorded link. Keep an open mind. This play is designed to make people laugh, and if an idea's funny, it's valid.

A Sense Of Period

In the original production, we opted for a period setting, circa 1930, choosing to ignore the resulting anachronisms. This is, of course, by no means essential to the plot, but it does lend a certain classic charm and character to the whole piece. Incidentally, you may find that it's easier to hire a period Police costume than it is to get hold of a modern one.

The period setting accounts for the use of the Victorian lamppost. While this is a nice touch, don't get too dispirited if, in the end, acquiring or making a suitable prop proves just too difficult. With the removal of one small reference to it in Act Two, the lamppost becomes optional.

A Word About Expletives

The more observant of you may notice the odd expletive and irreverent phrase. They are there for the sake of comedy. They are not there to offend, and it is our experience that they do not. This play has been throughly tested in front of live audiences.

However, you know best of all what is likely to be acceptable to your audiences, so if you feel you would like to soften the occasional word or phrase, by all means do so.

Properties

On Stage:

Victorian lamppost and walled area (backdrop for Plod's monologues)

Fireplace. *In it:* soot. *Near it:* companion set (no poker). *Above it:* mirror. *Above the mirror:* warthog's head.

Mantelpiece. *On it:* photograph of woman.

Waste-Paper Basket. *In it:* newspaper - headline "Evil Uncle In Boat Tragedy".

Bookshelves. *On them:* telephone and directory; scissors; vase and flowers; champagne bottle and two glasses; taxidermist's card; radio; water pistol; fizzy tablets; banana; newspaper.

Settee. *Near it:* table with chess set; Coffee table with pencil and diary. *Behind it:* cuddly teddy.

On back wall: 200 Club certificate; flying ducks (rigged to fall); photograph of Short's wife (rigged to rip wallpaper when removed).

Drinks table. *On it:* soda syphon; glasses; brandy; whiskey.

Side table. *On it;* newspaper - headline "Freak Hailstorm Here Last Night"; glass beaker with water.

Off-Stage - Props table:

Plod: *(Act One)* large plastic bag; head in bag; lab report; file. *(Act Two)* Exploded helmet and newspaper; black make-up; large photograph.

Drake: *(Act One)* chemistry set; false shirt front and tie. *(Act Two)* Violin and bow; Groucho disguise; wig.

Sabrina: *(Act One)* suitcase; mascara; wrapped-up fish; gun.

Dr Short: *(Act One)* doctor's bag; inside it: syringe.

Miss Short: suitcase; *inside it:* bag of broken pottery; piece of broken vase; orange, green, purple and brown handbag containing nail file.

Personal:

Plod: truncheon; notebook; pencil; sheet of paper and marker pen (for police sketch); small plastic bag; coins (one bent); watch.

Drake: pencil, coin, magnifying glass.

Dr Short: two wads of money; note "I'm coming to the house tonight".

Miss Short: handbag containing passport.

Production Notes

For more information on Flying Ducks Publications, write to *Flying Ducks Publications, Station Road, Highley, Shropshire* WV16 6NW.

ISBN 0 9517267 6 5

ACT ONE

Dramatic, sinister music sets the scene as the houselights go down. The next section could be pre-recorded, or acted out live. All we see are silhouetted figures - or possibly just shadows on the front curtain. One of the voices is that of Doctor Short. The other, his wife, could be played by any actress, as this is the first and only time she figures in the play. As we join the action, a terrible row is in progress.

Mrs Short What the hell's got into you tonight? Are you drunk?

Short No, not drunk. Intoxicated, perhaps. But not drunk.

Mrs Short You're behaving like a spoilt child.

Short Perhaps I'm just jealous.

Mrs Short Jealous? Jealous of what??

Short Jealous of me, of course.

Mrs Short Rupert, if this is some kind of sick joke, I'm afraid...

Short (*savagely vitriolic*) Jealous of my money. Jealous of my delightful country residence. Oh, not forgetting, of course, my dear friends - the most stomach-churningly "nice" circle of squares you could ever wish to meet at a golf club dinner.

Mrs Short Rupert - what's wrong? Why are you talking like this?

Short But jealous, perhaps most of all, of my beautiful wife. (*He grabs her wrist*)

Mrs Short Stop it! You're hurting me.

Short (*evilly menacing*) Oh, Victoria. Dear, sweet Victoria. Sugar-coated spouse of the good and respectable country doctor. You still don't get it, do you?

Mrs Short (*distressed and crying*) Rupert...you're frightening me.

Short Did you honestly think I was just going to sit back and let you have it all?

Mrs Short (*a moment's pause*) Oh, my God!

Short At last! The penny drops into its tiny slot. You always were stupid, Victoria.

Mrs Short But...you're dead.

Short No, my dear. You are.

A Flying Ducks Publication

The silhouetted figure of Short raises a poker menacingly into the air. The woman screams. Lights to black. Then, on one front corner of the stage, a lamppost gently illuminates the Police Sergeant standing below.

Plod The perfect crime. Never thought I'd hear myself say the words. Twenty-five years I've spent under this helmet, man and boy. Thought I'd seen it all. Until that night. Murder is never a pleasant business. Especially for the one who's been murdered. But there's one thing that we in the force could always count on. Somewhere, somehow, the villain would made a mistake. Sure as eggs is eggs. The strand of hair, the dropped cigarette end, the shred of torn clothing, the fingerprint. After all, nobody's perfect. Or are they? Once in a lifetime, once in a thousand years, Nature plays a terrible trick on all of us. It's the nightmare that we in the force all dread. Coming face to face with a man who is possessed not only with the heart of a devil, but also the mind of a genius. A man capable of planning, and committing...the perfect murder. So, what if there is no strand of hair? What if there is no cigarette end, no shred of torn clothing, no fingerprint? What if this man taunts you with his crime. Dares you to take on his brilliant, twisted mind. Well then, there really is only one last hope. To pit genius against genius. Good against evil. And, as the titanic battle of wills unfolds, a humble Police Sergeant can only stand...and marvel!

Dramatic music swells, and the lights fade up to reveal Doctor Short, standing in his lounge.

Short Sergeant. Thank you for coming so quickly.
Plod It's an unfortunate habit of mine, sir.
Short May I offer you a cup of tea?
Plod No thank you, sir. Not while I'm on duty.
Short Something stronger, perhaps - a glass of whiskey?
Plod Well, just a medium-sized one, then.
Short (*pouring a drink*) I er...I expect you're wondering why I sent for you.
Plod No, sir.
Short Very well, I'll tell you.

Plod is standing admiring a mounted warthog's head on the wall. Short moves up behind him.

Short It's my wife, Sergeant.

Plod Is it really, sir? Well, if you don't mind me saying so, you did the right thing.

Short What?

Plod (*gesturing to the warthog*) Always fancied something like that for 'er indoors - haven't got the name of the bloke who did it, have you?

Short Oh, the taxidermist. Rogers. Frank Rogers. I think I've got his card somewhere...there you go.

Plod Thank you very much, sir. Well, g'night, sir.

Short Er, Sergeant, can we get to the point?

Plod Point, sir?

Short The reason you're here.

Plod You sent for me, sir.

Short That's right.

Plod Why was that exactly?

Short Nice to see you're beginning to ask searching questions.

Plod Just doing my job, sir.

Short Indeed.

Plod Well, g'night, sir.

Short Sergeant, I haven't finished! My wife has gone missing.

Plod (*glancing at the warthog*) That wouldn't be your first wife then, sir?

Short As a matter of fact it isn't. How did you know that?

Plod I like to stay alert, sir.

Short Anyway, the fact remains, she's disappeared.

Plod When did you last see her?

Short Just before she disappeared.

Plod And you haven't seen her since?

Short Not to my knowledge.

Plod Mmm. Perhaps I'd better take a few particulars, sir.

Short That would be nice.

Plod Fire away, sir.

Short With what?

Plod Some particulars, sir.

Short Any particulars in particular, Sergeant?

Plod Let's start with the name, shall we, sir?

Short Short. Victoria Short.

Plod And your wife's name?

Short My wife's name is Victoria Short.

Plod That must get very confusing, sir.

Short Only to a policeman. Shall we start again, Sergeant?

Plod I think that would be wise, sir.

Short My name is Doctor Rupert Short. My wife's name is Victoria Short. It's easy to tell us apart. I'm here, she's missing.

Plod Missing? Perhaps I'd better take a few particulars.

Short (*through gritted teeth*) Whatever you say, Sergeant.

Plod Can you give me a description, sir?

Short (*this line should be customized to match a description of Plod*) Yes, about five feet ten, thirteen stone, balding, with a little black Hitler moustache.

Plod No, I meant a description of your wife.

Short That was a description of my wife.

Plod Oh. Are you sure you want me to find her, sir?

Short I'm pulling your leg, Sergeant. (*Pointing to a framed photograph on the wall*) Actually, my wife is very beautiful.

Plod Is that her, sir?

Short No. That's just a photograph of her. She's actually much bigger than that.

Plod And presumably she's also in colour.

Short Yes.

Plod holds a piece of paper against the wall next to the photograph, and begins to sketch a ridiculously naive picture.

Short What are you doing?

Plod Police sketch, sir. I'll have this circulated around the village.

Short Well that should do the trick. It's an uncanny likeness.

Plod Thank you, sir.

Short Look, why don't you just take the photograph?

Plod May I, sir?

Short Of course.

Plod unceremoniously takes the photograph from the wall. In doing so, he tears off a large strip of wallpaper, which remains attached to the frame.

Plod I'll file a report with our missing person's department - I'm sure she'll show up sooner or later, one way or another, dead or alive. Well, g'night, sir.

Short Is there nothing else you can do?

Plod Like what?

Short Well aren't you at least going to conduct a search?

Plod If you say she's not here, sir, I believe you.

A Flying Ducks Publication

Short Not of the house, you buffoon! Of the country!
Plod All right, all right, sir. Calm down. I know you're under stress. But it's not going to get us very far if you go around calling me a baboon, is it sir?
Short I did not call you a baboon, Sergeant. I called you a buffoon.
Plod A wind instrument?
Short That's a bassoon.
Plod Give up.
Short A clown, Sergeant. I called you a clown.
Plod Oh, right. Well, g'night, sir.
Short Sergeant! Look, I'm a very wealthy man. If you can pull a few strings, I'd be...extremely grateful.
Plod Are you trying to offer me a bribe, sir?
Short Good Heavens, no!
Plod Are you trying to offer me a bribe, sir?
Short Good Heavens, yes.
Plod How much?
Short A hundred.
Plod Two hundred.
Short One fifty.
Plod Done.

Short hands Plod a wad of notes.

Short I want the top man, Sergeant. Do you hear me? The best.
Plod Can I use your phone, sir? I'd like to call Scotland Yard.
Short Of course.
Plod Do you happen to know the code for Scotland from here, sir?
Short I think you'll find Scotland Yard is actually in London, Sergeant.
Plod *(after eyeing him up suspiciously, he finally smiles)* You're pulling my leg again, sir!
Short No, honestly. Here, let me get the number for you. *(He finds the number in a directory and shows Plod)* There, you see.
Plod Lord love a duck! Whatever will they think of next! *(He dials the number and conducts a ridiculously short muttered conversation, after which Plod seems in a state of mild shock)*
Short Well?
Plod Amazing.
Short What?
Plod I never thought they'd agree.

Short Agree to what?
Plod You asked for the top man, sir.
Short And?
Plod They're sending...him, sir.
Short Him?
Plod Oh, you're a lucky man, sir.
Short I am?
Plod He's a genius.
Short A genius, you say?
Plod He doesn't usually handle missing persons cases, but, well, I had to tell a little porky.
Short Just tell me who it is, Sergeant!
Plod Inspector Drake, sir.

A short drone of dramatic music, as the lights fade to a tight centre spotlight on Short.

Short Drake! Well, well. It couldn't have worked out better. The legendary Inspector Drake. What a fascinating challenge.
Plod *(stepping into the spotlight)* Sorry, sir?
Short Nothing. *(Lights back up)* I look forward to meeting him.
Plod He'll be here at ten o'clock, sir.
Short Until tomorrow then...
Plod Tonight, sir.
Short Erm, I don't think so, Sergeant. It's ten now.
Plod Not quite, sir.
Short Well, nevertheless, Sergeant, he won't be here by ten o'clock.
Plod Inspector Drake is never late, sir.
Short I admire your loyalty, Sergeant, but I'm sure we'll forgive him if he is a little late.
Plod *(sitting on the settee)* Inspector Drake is never late, sir.
Short Would you like to bet me...one hundred and fifty pounds that Drake will not be here by ten o'clock, Sergeant?
Plod No, sir.
Short I thought not.
Plod I'd like to bet you two hundred pounds he won't be late, sir.
Short Intriguing. *(He checks his watch, peeks out of the curtained windows, and produces another wad of notes from his pocket)* Very well, you're on. *(Sitting on the settee)* What time do you make it, Sergeant?

Plod Eight seconds to ten, sir.
Short Seven, six, five, four, three...(*he looks around, and smiles*). You owe me
  two hundred pounds, Sergeant.

*Drake pops up from underneath the middle cushion of the settee (see production
notes). He immediately snatches the money from Short's hand, and pockets it.*

Drake I think not. (*He hands a coin to Plod*) Your usual commission, Sergeant.
Plod Thank you, sir.
Short (*recovering from the shock*) How do you do. I'm Short.
Drake (*refusing the handshake*) How do you do. I'm quite tall. Excuse us -
  police business. (*Aside, to Plod*) All right, Sergeant - what have you got?
Plod Nasty one, sir. The geezer over there reckons his name's Victoria, sir.
Drake Victoria?
Plod It gets worse, sir. He reckons that's his first wife.
Drake It's a warthog, Sergeant.
Plod Yes, sir.
Drake A dead warthog.
Plod Very much so, sir.
Drake It's going to be one of those nights. I can sense it.
Plod Do you think he's lying?
Drake Who would lie about being married to a warthog?
Plod Exactly, sir.
Drake All right. What do we know about her?
Plod She's a warthog, sir.
Drake Apart from the fact that she's a warthog.
Plod She's dead, sir.
Drake Apart from the fact that she's a dead warthog.
Plod Very little, sir.
Drake Name?
Plod Plod, sir. Sergeant Plod.
Drake Not you! Her!
Plod Oh, er...Victoria, sir.
Drake They're both called Victoria?
Plod Yes, sir. Then there's the second wife, er...
Drake Don't tell me - her name is Victoria.
Plod Hah. No, sir!
Drake Good.
Plod (*checking his notes*) Oh, yes, sir!

A Flying Ducks Publication

Drake Let's simplify this, shall we, Sergeant? Apart from us two, is everyone else involved in this case called Victoria?

Plod Yes, sir.

Drake Right.

Plod Apart from Frank.

Drake Who's Frank?

Plod The taxi driver, sir.

Drake Go on.

Plod He's the one who mounted her and stuffed her.

Drake A taxi driver called Frank mounted her and stuffed her.

Plod Yes, sir. And judging by the look on her face, I reckon it was the last thing he did before she died.

Drake So let me get this straight. We have a man called Vicky, who's married to a warthog, also called Vicky. She is accosted by a taxi driver called Frank, who mounts her, and stuffs her. Meanwhile, Vicky's second wife, also called Vicky, disappears.

Plod And who can blame her, sir? She takes one look at what happened to the first wife, and scarpers. Open and shut case.

Drake I think I'll come in again, Sergeant.

Plod Right, sir.

Short Perhaps I could explain, Inspector...

Drake Ah, Vicky.

Short Rupert. Doctor Rupert Short. My wife is Victoria.

Drake Your wife is not the issue here, Doctor. All right, Rupert... Rupe... Ru... Rr... Let's establish a few groundrules here. First of all, I don't like you. But I'm going to put up with you because I have a job to do. It's not a pleasant job, but someone's got to do it, and I expect nothing less than your total cooperation.

(He pronounces the word as coop-eration, rather than co-operation)

Short What the hell are you talking about, Inspector?

Drake What the hell I are talking about, Vicky, is murder. In case it has escaped your notice, a violent crime has been committed here.

Short Has it?

Drake Hasn't it?

Plod I don't know, sir.

Drake Get over here, Sergeant. *(Aside)* Why am I here?

Plod Nobody else was available, sir.

Drake What's going on? Come on, out with it.

Plod *(sulkily)* His wife's disappeared.

Drake A missing person's case?

A Flying Ducks Publication

Plod Yes, sir.
Drake I don't do missing persons.
Plod But sir...
Drake I don't do missing persons, Sergeant! I only do murders. Would you like me to turn this into a murder?
Plod No, sir.
Drake Right, that's it. I'm going home.
Plod Please, sir! Take the case! Just this once.
Drake (*suspicious*) Why?
Plod He was...most insistent, sir.
Drake How much?
Plod Sorry, sir?
Drake The bribe - how much?
Plod What bribe?
Drake Two hundred.
Plod One hundred.
Drake One fifty.
Plod Yes, sir.
Drake Hand it over.
Plod But sir...
Drake Hand it over! (*He does*) And the small change.
Plod But sir...
Drake Empty your pockets. Now!

Plod hands over some small change, including a bent penny, which Drake examines and hands back.

Drake If there's one thing I can't stand it's a bent copper. All right, Sergeant. Ten minutes. If there's no sign of a murder by half past ten, I'm going home.
Plod Right, sir.
Drake Vicky! I think perhaps we got off on the wrong foot.
Short Perhaps you should know from the outset, Inspector, I do not tolerate fools gladly.
Drake Then boy, are you in for a rough evening. (*Short starts checking his appearance in the mirror above the fireplace. Drake looks up at the warthog*) Handsome beast.
Short Thank you, Inspector. You're not so bad yourself.
Drake I meant the warthog.
Short Tease.

Drake   Where did you two first meet?
Short   On holiday in Canada.
Drake   Tell me, did she...er, did she die of natural causes?
Short   Of course not. I shot her.
Drake   (*Aside*)   All right, Sergeant, I'm staying.

The phone rings, and Plod silently answers it.

Short   Could we actually concentrate on the business in hand?
Drake   Which is?
Short   Finding my wife.
Drake   Ah, yes. (*Picking up a photograph on the mantelpiece*)   The missing wife.
Short   That's my daughter, Sabrina.
Drake   No, that's just a photograph of her.
Short   Touche.
Drake   Where's the real thing?
Short   In Canada.   While we were over there on holiday she fell in love with a
   Mountie called Mervin.   Married him and never came home.   That was three
   years ago.
Plod   Sir.
Drake   Yes, Sergeant?
Plod   It's Inspector Morse, sir.
Drake   Excuse me. (*Urgently taking the receiver*)   Yes, Morse.

We hear a short morse code statement, and Drake slams down the receiver.

Drake   Bloody hoax calls. Sergeant?
Plod   Sir?
Drake   No more calls.
Plod   Right sir.   (*Plod immediately produces a pair of scissors and
   unceremoniously cuts through the telephone wire, unseen by Drake.   Then,
   Drake turns*)
Drake   Unless it's extremely urgent.
Plod   Yes, sir. (*Plod sheepishly looks at the wire, and begins trying to tie the ends
   back together*)
Drake   Right - to work. (*He takes out a magnifying glass, with which he proceeds
   to scour the room.   He finally settles on examining a certificate on the wall*)
   The 200 Club. What's this?
Short   That, Inspector, is one of the world's most exclusive clubs.   It's an elite

branch of Mensa - to be a member you have to have an IQ of 200 or more. There are only four of us in the country.

Drake Oh, so you and the Sergeant already knew each other?

Plod Sorry, sir?

Drake Never mind. (*Spotting a bottle of champagne and two glasses*) Expecting company?

Short I was rather hoping my wife might return.

Drake (*spotting a chess board with a game in progress*) And is she your chess opponent?

Short Victoria? Yes, sometimes. She is an exceptional player, by normal standards. But I'm afraid the only person capable of giving me a really stimulating game...is myself.

Drake You play with yourself?

Short When Victoria's not in the mood, yes. What about you?

Drake Never!

Short I bet I could mate you in three moves.

Drake You just bloody try it, mate.

Short It's my one great weakness, Inspector. I'm obsessed with games of logic. Chess. Backgammon. Ker-Plunk. I yearn to pit my wits against a worthy opponent. But for the last few years it's been getting very boring. You see, Inspector, I always, always win. (*He makes a chess move*)

Drake (*retaliating with a move*) So do I.

Short What a fascinating scenario. If we play against each other, one of us must lose.

Drake That's right.

Short So, what's your favourite game, Inspector?

Drake Murder.

Short An interesting choice. I must challenge you some time. (*He makes another move on the chess board. From now on, Drake and Short will take it in turns at key moments to make a move, setting up the idea of a challenge between them*) Your move.

Drake Mmm. (*Thoughtfully making his move*) Your wife had blonde shoulder-length hair, and a strawberry-coloured mole on her back.

Short Good Lord, how did you know that?

Drake I slept with her last week. Just my little joke, Doctor. Actually, I deduced it from this entry in your wife's diary. (*He picks up a diary from a coffee table, and reads from it*) "November 14th - made an appointment to have my blonde shoulder-length hair cut. It's now almost down to the strawberry-coloured mole on my back". Sergeant - this is important evidence.

A Flying Ducks Publication

The Sergeant produces a small plastic bag, into which Drake attempts to put the diary. The bag is slightly too small, despite Drake's attempts to stretch it.

Drake Has your wife got a smaller diary?
Short No.
Drake Get a larger bag, Sergeant.
Plod Sir.

Exit Plod. Drake notices something behind the settee, and stoops to examine it.

Drake Spilled something down your settee, Vicky?
Short What? Oh, yes, I did spill a little coffee over it the other evening. I tried everything to get the stains out. In the end I used bleach. Made rather a mess of it, I'm afraid.
Drake Yes. Haven't you just. Ah, Sergeant. *(Plod has entered, with a huge plastic bag, approximately four feet square, into which Drake pops the diary)* And the pencil. *(Plod pops the pencil into the bag)* We'd better take the table as well. *(They put the coffee table into the bag)* Run that past the boys in the lab. See what they come up with.
Plod Right, sir.
Drake And see if you can find this taxi driver · what was his name?
Plod Vicky, sir. No, Frank.
Drake Frank. Put out an APB.
Plod What's an APB, sir?
Drake Sergeant, you're a policeman! Surely you know what an APB is!
Plod Why don't you remind me, sir.
Drake *(struggling)* All right, let's not worry about that now. Just get cracking.
Plod Sir.
Drake Oh, and Sergeant. *(Aside)* The 200 Club.
Plod Oh, yes, sir. The exclusive branch of Mensa. To be a member you have to have an IQ of 200 or more.
Drake How did you know that?
Plod I entered for it last year, sir. I did quite well actually.
Drake Really.
Plod Yes, sir. Apparently they only failed me on the mental part of the exam.
Drake Shame. Anyway, there are only four members in the country. He's one of them...
Plod And you want me to find out who the other two are.
Drake I knew I could rely on you, Sergeant.

A Flying Ducks Publication

Plod   Consider it done, sir.

Exit Plod, with bag and contents.

Drake   (*examining the fireplace, he emerges with a blackened nose*)   Been having a fire, Vicky?

Short   Yes, I had a fire last night, as a matter of fact.

Drake   Isn't it a little warm for fires?

Short   On the contrary.   If you check the weather report you'll see that we had a freak hail storm here last night.

Short hands Drake a newspaper.   The large headline reads "Freak Hailstorm Here Last Night".   Disgruntled, he discards the newspaper.   He flicks on a radio just long enough to hear the words "freak hailstorm here last..." and then switches it off peevishly.

Drake   Mmm.   (*Checking the fire's companion set*)   The poker.

Short   What about it?

Drake   It's missing.   (*He makes a quick chess move*)

Short   You're very observant, Inspector.

Drake   It's my job to be observ...arrgh!

Drake, walking forward, has fallen off the front of the stage.   Plod re-enters with the plastic bag and contents, plus a lab report.

Plod   Sir?

Drake   (*bouncing up, casually*)   Well everything seems okay down here.   Ah, Sergeant!   (*He stretches out his hand for Plod to help him up.   Plod tugs at his sleeve, and falls back as the arm of Drake's jacket comes completely off in his hands*)   Interesting room you've got here, Vicky.

Short   You should try the steps next time.   Well, I have work to do.   If you need me, Inspector, I'll be in the library.

Short exits.   Drake proceeds back on stage via the steps.

Drake   What's the news, Sergeant?

Plod   Pretty much as we thought, sir.   Here's the lab report.   It confirms our suspicions.   A diary, a pencil, and a coffee table.

Drake   Mmm.   What's that fourth item?

Plod Er...plastic bag, sir.
Drake Thorough as ever, eh? All right, put the table and the pencil back. I'll
  hang on to the diary. You never know, there might be some rude bits in it.
Plod I'm afraid not, sir.
Drake All right, bin it.
Plod Oh, I've also started interviewing all taxi drivers in the area, sir. So far,
  none by the name of Frank.
Drake How many have you asked?
Plod One, sir.
Drake And his name wasn't Frank.
Plod No, sir. Well, I don't think so. That's one question I forgot to ask him.
Drake Stick at it, Sergeant.
Plod Sir.
Drake Oh, Sergeant. Any news on the 200 Club?
Plod (*consulting his notebook*) Oh, yes sir. Very strange. According to official
  records, there are only three members, not four. There's a Doctor Rupert Short,
  whoever he might be, some woman, and an old git, sir.
Drake And that's what the official Mensa records said, is it, Sergeant? Some
  woman and an old git.
Plod That was the gist of it, sir.
Drake But definitely only three people?
Plod Yes, sir.
Drake Mmm. I wonder why he said there were four?
Plod Perhaps he can't count, sir.
Drake Thank you, Sergeant.

*Drake discovers a beaker with colourless liquid in it on a side table. He sniffs at
it suspiciously. Short enters.*

Short I wouldn't touch that if I were you.
Drake What is it?
Short Highly concentrated sulphuric acid.
Drake Sergeant. (*He beckons Plod over*) Thirsty?
Short I wouldn't, Drake. It will kill him.
Drake He enjoys his work. Sergeant, could you lend me a hand?
Plod Of course, sir.
Drake Good man. (*Drake grabs Plod's hand and plunges it into the container.
  It bubbles, courtesy of some fizzy soluble aspirins Plod is holding, as Plod
  writhes in agony. Drake continues to hold Plod's hand in the liquid, as he talks*

casually to Short). Tell me, Doctor. What would this stuff do to metal?
Short Dissolve it, of course.
Drake Completely?
Short Yes. Given time.
Drake Forgive me if this sounds like a stupid question, but why have you got a beaker of sulphuric acid in the house?
Short It is a stupid question, Inspector, but I will forgive you. I'm a scientist, I work with all manner of chemicals.
Drake *(finally letting the agonized Plod remove his hand)* All right, Sergeant, thank you.

Plod thrusts his hand into a vase of flowers for relief, and in the process gets his hand stuck in the vase. Enter Sabrina, with a suitcase.

Sabrina Hello, daddy.
Short Sabrina! What the hell are you doing here?
Sabrina I've left Mervin. I couldn't stand it any more.
Short What happened?
Sabrina I found him in bed with an elk. He said they were only petting, but frankly it crushed my self confidence. You were right, daddy - I should never have married him. I've come home.
Short Sabrina, this really isn't a good time.
Sabrina Daddy...what's wrong? What's this policeman doing here?
Short Darling, it's your mother.
Sabrina This policeman's my mother?
Short No, Inspector Drake and the Sergeant are here to help look for your mother.
Sabrina Victoria? What's happened to her?
Short We don't know, darling. She's...disappeared.
Sabrina Disappeared?
Short I'm sorry.
Sabrina Uhh! *(She faints)*
Drake Sergeant - brandy.
Plod Sir!

Plod tries to pour a brandy, but is hampered severely by the vase stuck on his hand.

Short I'll do it.

Short pours a glass of brandy and rushes it to Drake, who swigs it off instantly.

Drake That's better. Now, call a doctor.
Plod Right, sir.
Short I'll get my bag.

Short exits. Plod tries to phone a doctor, but quickly realizes he's cut the telephone wire, and puts the receiver down sheepishly.

Drake Did you call a doctor?
Plod Er...
Short (*rushing in with a doctor's bag*) I'm a doctor!
Drake Good work, Sergeant! Now give me a hand.

They struggle to lift her up. Meanwhile, Short prepares a large syringe.

Drake On the settee, Sergeant.
Plod Right sir.

Plod drops Sabrina and sits on the settee.

Drake Not you! Her!
Plod Oh, right sir.

They eventually get her onto the settee, and Short prepares to inject her.

Drake What's that?
Short Just a light sedative.
Drake Oh no you don't!
Short What the hell do you think you're doing?

A struggle ensues between Short and Drake, which culminates in Plod, who is bending over trying to free his hand, getting the syringe jabbed into his bottom. The impact causes him to pluck his hand from the vase, and he is left, eyes bulging, holding the flowers. From that moment he begins staggering around the stage, desperately trying to stay on his feet under the influence of the injection. The syringe is dropped on the floor.

Short Now look what you've done!

A Flying Ducks Publication

Drake She's coming round.

Sabrina I'm all right. Leave me alone. I just want to know what's happened to Victoria.

Short I'm sorry you had to find out this way. If I'd only known you were coming...

Sabrina I tried telephoning from the station, but I think the phone must be out of order.

Drake Check that, would you, Sergeant?

Plod (*barely conscious*) Er, right, sir.

Sabrina Daddy, aren't you pleased to see me?

Short Of course I am, I'm just...tired, that's all. It's been an exhausting day.

Sabrina I can imagine. The Sergeant looks shattered.

Short If you don't mind, Inspector, I'm going to retire.

Drake It's nice to know you can afford it.

Short Sabrina will see you out. Do keep me in touch with your progress, Inspector.

Drake (*with sinister undertones*) Don't worry, Vicky, when I find out what happened to your wife, you'll be the first to know.

Short (*smiling*) Your move, Inspector.

Short exits. Plod finally collapses over the back of the settee, ignored by everyone.

Sabrina (*after he has exited, feeling dejected*) Goodnight, father.

Drake He was obviously pleased to see you.

Sabrina I've never seen him like this before. He's behaving very strangely.

Drake Did you two part on bad terms?

Sabrina On the contrary. I've always been very close to my father. Well, as close as you can be on the other side of the world. (*Looking at Plod*) Is he all right?

Drake I don't know. Drink?

Sabrina Shouldn't you do something?

Drake Like what?

Sabrina What about mouth-to-mouth resuscitation?

Drake I'd rather French kiss the warthog.

Sabrina It's a boar.

Drake Yes, isn't it just. (*Passing her a drink*) Besides, if there's any mouth-to-mouth going on around here, I'd rather you be at the other end.

Sabrina Oh, Inspector. You don't waste any time, do you?

Drake Not where rumpy pumpy is concerned.

A Flying Ducks Publication

Drake closes in to kiss her.

Plod Get in there, son!
Drake (*drawing away*) Feeling better, Sergeant?
Plod Yes, sir.
Drake Right, I've got a job for you. (*He picks up the syringe*) I want you to get this analyzed.
Plod It's a syringe, sir.
Drake Yes I know it's a syringe! I want to know what was in it!
Plod Oh, I'm not sure I'm up to riding my bicycle at the moment, sir. I'm still feeling a little dopey.
Drake Well if we wait for that to clear up we'll all die of old age. God, look at him. A half wit on half power. A quarter wit.
Plod I'll have a go, sir.
Drake Never mind, I'll do it myself. Wait here - and don't let her out of your sight.
Plod Right sir.
Drake If I'm not back in five minutes...wait another five minutes.

Exit Drake. Sabrina pours Plod a drink.

Sabrina Here, drink this. It will make you feel better.
Plod Thank you, Miss.
Sabrina He's an interesting man, your Inspector friend.
Plod The best, Miss.
Sabrina Do you think he can find my mother?
Plod If anyone can, Miss. Mind if I help myself to another drink?
Sabrina Of course not.
Plod Tell me, Miss - did your father love your mother?
Sabrina Does a bear shit in the woods?
Plod Er, I'm not sure, Miss. I could probably find out for you.
Sabrina No, no. It's just an expression I picked up on my travels, Sergeant. It means "of course"...like erm..."Is the Pope Catholic".
Plod You've got me again, Miss.
Sabrina Never mind, Sergeant.

Enter Drake, with a child's chemistry set, from which he takes various beakers, test tubes, etc.

A Flying Ducks Publication

Drake Miss Short, I'll need your help.
Sabrina Of course.
Drake I need sodium chloride, some acetic acid...
Sabrina Oh, I don't think...
Drake Just common table salt, household vinegar...
Sabrina Right!
Drake And a large haddock.
Sabrina Coming up.

She exits.

Drake I'm starving. All right, Sergeant - let's see what we have here. *(Drake squirts the contents of the syringe into a beaker, and starts to perform a ludicrous series of tests on the liquid, with Plod taking notes)* Specific gravity, five point one.
Plod Five point one, sir.
Drake PH balance, seven point four five.
Plod Seven point four five, sir.
Drake Protein absorbtion ratio....eighty.....four.
Plod P.A.R...eighty-four, sir.
Drake No, no, no! Eighty-three.
Plod No, no, no, eighty-three, sir.
Drake Densitometer infusion suffix - eight to the power three.
Plod Eight to the power three, sir.
Drake Molecular viscosity...negative.
Plod Negative, sir.
Drake Right, Sergeant - what have we got?
Plod A complete load of bollocks, sir.
Drake Oh, bugger it. *(He swigs at the liquid, gargles, then spits it out into Plod's helmet)* Aha! A mild sedative, eh?
Plod Well, sir?
Drake Methyl Anti-Hystadine.
Plod Menthol Tetra-Chloradine?
Drake Precisely.
Sabrina *(re-entering with a wrapped-up fish)* Excuse my ignorance, Inspector, but what exactly is Tetryl Hexaphobadobadine?
Drake Poison. Just one drop of this Chlora Flora-testaclecleaner is enough to poleaxe a savage bull, or even slow down the Sergeant here. But this syringe was not intended for the Sergeant.

Plod You mean?

Drake That's precisely what I mean. (*Pause*) You don't know what I mean, do you?

Plod No, sir.

Sabrina I think I know what you mean, Inspector, and it's preposterous.

Drake I'm sorry to put it to you so bluntly, but I fear your father was trying to kill you.

Sabrina That's nonsense. It was a simple mistake.

Drake What's more, I think he may have murdered your mother.

Sabrina You're wrong, Drake, wrong. Do you hear me? I won't listen to any more of this nonsense!

Sabrina stuffs the fish into Drake's hands and storms out.

Drake Follow her, Sergeant!

Plod Right, sir.

Plod pops on his dripping helmet, exits sharply after Sabrina, and re-enters instantly.

Drake Well?

Plod She's sleeping, sir.

Drake (*picking up a chesspiece*) Poor kid. Just a pawn in a brutal game of draughts. (*Drake opens up his fish supper, only to find a whole, uncooked fish. He tosses it away*) Well, Sergeant. What do your guts tell you?

Plod That I shouldn't have had that third curry last night.

Drake Do you know what my guts tell me?

Plod No, sir.

Drake That he did it. He killed his wife. Brutally. Savagely. Clinically. Unemotionally. Cold bloodedly. And pre-meditatedivelively. I think he picked up the poker from the hearth, and with one, sudden, savage blow, sent it crashing down onto her defenceless body. (*He gives Plod the benefit of a demonstration, using his truncheon, which sends Plod plummeting down behind the settee*) This is where they were standing - right here - by the settee. He then coolly burnt all his bloodstained clothes in the hearth, bleached the stains from the settee, and dissolved the poker in acid. (*Drake passes behind the settee, lifting up as he walks on the unconscious Plod, who lets out a muted yelp*) Yes, I know what you're thinking, Sergeant. You're thinking, if he did murder her, why would he call in the Police to look for her? Logic, Sergeant.

A Flying Ducks Publication

He knew others would eventually notice her disappearance, and that then he'd be under immediate suspicion for not reporting it earlier. So, as soon as he was sure he'd removed all the clues, he called you in, and played the worried husband. (*He sits on the settee. Again Plod groans*) Yes, I know what you're saying, Sergeant. I'm only guessing. We have no proof. And something's not right. There's something missing.

Plod drags himself up and over the back of the settee, and makes an indistinct grunt.

Drake   That's right, Sergeant. Motive. (*Getting up and pacing around once again*) All right, let's examine what we have here, Sergeant. We have a missing woman - or rather, we don't have a missing woman, because she's missing. We have a daughter who arrives back unexpectedly from Canada, after demounting a Mountie. We have a doctor who tries to poison that daughter. We have a new poker, a jar of acid, a hearth full of charred ashes, and a bleached sofa. In short, Sergeant, we have all the ingredients of a murder. But what we do not have, is a reason why. What we do not have, is a motive.
Plod   What about murder, sir?
Drake   That's not a motive.
Plod   Isn't it?
Drake   No.
Plod   What is it, then?
Drake   Well it's a...it's a...it's a thing.
Plod   Oh, right, sir.
Drake   A motive's like, well, like money.
Plod   What about money, sir?
Drake   No. He's already a wealthy man.
Plod   Or hatred.
Drake   What about hatred?
Plod   No, sir. Not hatred.
Drake   You think he loved his wife, do you?
Plod   Does the Pope shit in the woods?
Drake   What?
Plod   Is a bear Catholic?
Drake   What the hell are you talking about, Sergeant?
Plod   Just expressions, sir. They mean "of course".
Drake   They mean "no".
Plod   Do they?

Drake Can you imagine the Head of the Catholic Church nipping behind a tree for a quick crap?

Plod I suppose not, sir.

Drake Or a giant, hairy grizzly bear saying three Hail Mary's?

Plod It sounded logical at the time.

Drake Stay away from logic, Sergeant. You haven't got the necessary equipment.

Plod What if they just had a row, sir, he lost his temper, and bashed her one?

Drake Maybe, Sergeant. But that doesn't explain why he should want to kill his own daughter. His own flesh and blood. No, Sergeant, whichever way you cut the mustard, it just doesn't stack up.

Plod Mustard, sir?

Drake No, thanks. No, this was no straightforward murder, Sergeant. There's something deeper going on here. And what we need is a clear-cut motive. (*A flash of inspiration*) What about sex, Sergeant?

Plod Is that an order, sir?

Drake No, Sergeant. What about sex - as a motive?

Plod How d'you mean, sir?

Drake Imagine you fell in love with a stunning, nubile young lady. Would that be enough to make you...

Plod Oh, yes, sir.

Drake Let me finish the question!

Plod Sorry, sir.

Drake Would that be enough to make you kill your wife?

Plod (*instantly*) Oh, yes, sir.

Drake (*again examining a chesspiece*) So, maybe there's another player in this evil game we've yet to meet. Sergeant, I want you to go upstairs...

Plod (*heading straight for the door*) Right, sir!

Drake Sergeant! Would you like to know why you're going upstairs?

Plod If you think it would help, sir.

Drake Yes, I think it would. Bear with me - it's not a long sentence.

Plod Right, sir.

Drake I want you to go upstairs, drag Vicky out of bed, and bring him here to me. I'd like another little chat with him.

Plod Right, sir.

Drake And Sergeant, remember he's innocent until proven guilty. I want him back here in one piece.

Plod exits just as Sabrina enters. She puts her finger to her lips, playfully beckoning Plod not to let on that she's in the room, as she wishes to surprise

Drake. She sneaks up behind Drake, who is bending to study the chessboard, and tweaks his bottom. Drake stops, stunned.

Drake One more stunt like that, Sergeant, and you'll be walking funny in the morning.
Sabrina I already walk funny.
Drake (*turning*) Oh, it's you.
Sabrina I came down to apologise.
Drake What for?
Sabrina For storming off like that. I realize you're just trying to do your job. But you're wrong, Inspector. You couldn't be more wrong. Ours is a very close family. My father wouldn't hurt a fly, let alone his own wife and daughter.
Drake If it's all the same to you, I'd like to keep an open mind on that.
Sabrina As you wish. (*Spotting the chess board*) Do you fancy a game?
Drake I'm already in the middle of one.
Sabrina You just don't like the idea of being beaten by a woman.
Drake Oh, I don't know. Look, I have to warn you. I've sent Sergeant Plod to get your father. He'll be down here any moment.
Sabrina Are you going to interrogate him?
Drake I have some more questions, yes.
Sabrina (*lasciviously*) And what about me? Are you going to probe me unmercifully?
Drake Maybe.
Sabrina And what if I don't co-operate?
Drake I could make it very hard for you.
Sabrina I was hoping you'd say that. Kiss me.

Their lips are about to meet, when Plod pops his head round the door.

Plod Er, sir.
Drake (*patiently, belying his inner fury*) Ah, Sergeant. Any luck?
Plod Not as much as you, by the look of it. Can I have a word, sir - in private?
Sabrina It's all right, Sergeant. I was just leaving.
Plod Sorry, Miss. Police business.
Sabrina That's quite all right. Goodnight.
Plod (*entering slowly. He is carrying an opaque plastic bag containing something hidden behind his back*) Hope I wasn't interrupting anything, sir.
Drake (*putting his arm around him*) Not at all, Sergeant.
Short (*reaching the door*) Goodnight.

A Flying Ducks Publication

Drake/Plod (*cheerfully*) Goodnight!

Exit Sabrina. As the door clicks shut, Drake's arm tightens on Plod's neck.

Drake Don't you ever...ever...do that again! D'you hear me?
Plod Yes, sir!
Drake You bastard! That's the nearest I've got to getting my leg over in years!
Plod It's important sir.
Drake Nothing...nothing, is more important that me getting my leg over - understand?
Plod Yes sir!
Drake Now, where's Doctor Shortarse?
Plod He wasn't in his room, sir.
Drake Then search the rest of the house!
Plod I did, sir.
Drake And you couldn't find him.
Plod Oh, I found him all right.
Drake Then where is he?
Plod In the wine cellar, sir.
Drake Drunk, eh?
Plod No sir. Dead!

Plod swings round with a dramatic look-to-front, as if he's expecting a music stab and spotlight. Drake taps him on the shoulder.

Drake Timing, Sergeant.

Drake swings round, and there's a music stab and spotlight.

Drake Dead?
Plod Yes sir.
Drake Are you sure?
Plod Well, I can't be absolutely certain, sir, because it was pretty dark down there, and I only managed to find the head. (*Producing and opening the bag*) But I reckon he's a goner.
Drake Uggh! What's happened to it?
Plod Very nasty, sir. It's been sliced into four equal pieces.
Drake Oh, that reminds me, I must phone headquarters. (*He tries the phone*) Damn. Phone's dead too. Get over there straight away, Sergeant. Arrange for

the head to be taken away and examined. Have your own done while you're at it. And bring me back everything we have on this Doctor Rupert Vicky Short.
Plod   Right, sir.
Drake   I'm going to break the bad news to his daughter.

Music. Spotlight on Plod, still holding the head in the bag.

Plod   So, amateur sleuths, what looked like an open and shut case - man murders wife with poker - suddenly has a bit of a nasty twist. Not only do we have an attempted murder on the daughter, apparently without a motive, but also the prime suspect for all these dirty deeds, Doctor Rupert Short himself, now comes in kit form. One thing's for sure, he's not going to be causing us any more trouble. *(The spotlight fades momentarily, then comes back up)* Or is he?

Spotlight down, music. As the lights come up, Sabrina is wailing uncontrollably on Drake's shoulder. He is comforting her.

Drake   There, there now. Come on. Yes, I know. It's all right. Shhh. Just try to relax......Shut up!!!!

Sabrina, shocked into silence by Drake's final outburst, moves away from him, revealing a disastrous mess of mascara over her face. A disgruntled Drake looks down at his white shirt, which is now plastered in make-up.

Sabrina   I'm sorry. *(Drake tears off the shirt and tie. There's another identical shirt and tie underneath)*   First mother disappears. Then you accuse father of trying to kill me. And now he's...(*she breaks down again, rushes to Drake, and Sabrina blows her nose on his new shirt*). I'm all right. Drake - it's now more important than ever that I clear my father's name. He's no murderer.
Drake   Are you sure?
Sabrina   I'd stake my life on it.
Drake   You almost did.
Sabrina   He's my father, damn it. He's wasn't capable of hurting anyone.
Drake   Not even in a fit of passion.
Sabrina   Never!
Drake   Perhaps he and your mother had a row...
Sabrina   No!!
Drake   Perhaps he just lost his head. *(Sabrina wails)* Oh, I'm sorry, I didn't mean...all right, all right. Look, there's something I have to say to you - it's

going to seem very callous, but I have to say it.

Sabrina What?

Drake Well, the circumstances surrounding your father's death - the way we found him - lead me to believe that it was not suicide.

Sabrina So?

Drake So, that leads me to the inexorable conclusion that it might have been murder. Are you following me so far?

Sabrina Perfectly.

Drake Well, as you were the only other one in the house at the time...

Sabrina Oh! Well that takes the biscuit! That really does put the icing on the cake. That just about wraps it up in fancy paper and puts a little pretty-coloured bow on it, doesn't it, Drake?

Drake Does it?

Sabrina First you claim my father tried to murder me - now you're saying I murdered him!

Drake Look, there's no need to take it personally.

Sabrina Just who the hell do you think you are?

Drake (*angry*) I'll tell you who the hell I think I are, shall I? I are the detective what's going to solve this case. And let me tell you exactly how I'm going to do it. First of all I take a man who's alive one minute, and dead the next. Then, I add up all the people in the house who could have done it - you, me, the Sergeant. Then, I take away the policemen. That leaves you. And let me tell you something else, Miss La-di-bloody-da Sabrina Shortbread. I don't feel sorry for murderers just because they're women - especially women who ruin my favourite shirt!

Sabrina You're so sexy when you're angry.

Drake Then marry me!

Sabrina Yes! (*They fall in a passionate hug*) Oh, yes!

Drake I'm sorry.

Sabrina So am I.

Drake Did you kill him?

Sabrina No.

Drake Good. I had to ask.

Sabrina I know. (*Walking away from the hug*) Oh, Drake! I can't believe all this is happening.

Drake (*pouring a whiskey*) Believe it, doll.

Sabrina Look at the state of me. I must look dreadful.

Drake Beauty is in the eye of the beholder. To me, you look...(*he looks up at her*)...reasonably okay.

Sabrina How can you stay so cool? I'm a wreck!
Drake Here, drink this. It'll calm your nerves.

He hands the drink to Sabrina. His hand is shaking so much most of it ends up on the floor.

Sabrina Thanks. So, now how do you explain my father's death?
Drake Well, if you didn't do it, there's only one other explanation.
Sabrina The Sergeant?
Drake No. Whoever did this had brains. Don't you see? It's the perfect crime. You can't be accused of murder if you're dead.
Sabrina You've lost me.
Drake Who's the only other person who had access to the house?
Sabrina Well, no-one.
Drake Your mother!
Sabrina My mother?
Drake She could have set this up to look as if she'd been murdered, and then sneaked in to kill your father. She could also have changed the serum in your father's case for poison. It all fits.
Sabrina Inspector. In the last ten minutes, you've accused my father of murdering my mother and trying to murder me, you've accused me of murdering my father, and now you're accusing my mother of murdering my father and trying to poison me. If we're to be married, I really think you should have more respect for my family.
Drake It's a crazy mixed up jig-saw of a world out there, doll. I'm just trying to put all the pieces back in the frame in the right order to form one big piece.
Sabrina *(bemused)* What?
Drake Nothing.
Sabrina Look, I'd better tell you - you'd find out anyway sooner or later. My mother is not my mother.
Drake She's not?
Sabrina No.
Drake Whose mother is she then?
Sabrina She's not anyone's mother. My real mother died when I was very young. My father re-married.
Drake I see.
Sabrina Three times.
Drake Three times?
Sabrina Yes. This is his fourth.

A Flying Ducks Publication

Drake What happened to them?

Sabrina They just kept...popping off.

Drake Popping off??

Sabrina Well, dying. All very innocent. My father was just unlucky with women. He attracted them like flies, of course, being rich, but, well, he just never picked a winner.

Drake This plot, rather like a certain police Sergeant I know, is getting thicker by the minute.

Sabrina Look - none of that changes my view about Victoria - that's my current step-mother, well, current if she's still alive. She's a good woman. And she loved him, I'm sure of it.

Drake Well, one thing's for sure. Whoever did it, they're not going to get away with it. I'll track them down, even if it takes me the rest of my life.

Sabrina Oh, Drake! Kiss me.

Drake What, now?

Sabrina Yes, now. I want to count your fillings with my tongue.

Drake Grrrrrr!

Their lips are about to join, as Plod enters.

Plod Can I have a word, sir? It's important.

Drake, exasperated, whimpers, then moves away and pours himself a large whiskey.

Sabrina Sergeant, come in. I'd like you to be the first to know. The Inspector and I are going to be married.

Plod Married? But he's already mar...(*Plod's revelation is stopped mid-sentence as the contents of Drake's glass forcefully hit his face*)

Drake You were saying, Sergeant?

Plod Nothing, sir.

Drake Now, what's so desperately important that it couldn't have waited two minutes?

Sabrina Two minutes?

Drake At least.

Plod Can I have a word in private, sir?

Drake (*to Sabrina*) Keep it warm, doll. (*He leads Plod to the front of the stage*) This had better be good, Sergeant.

Plod The head, sir.

Drake What about the head?

Plod I've lost it, sir.
Drake You've lost it.
Plod Yes, sir.
Drake What do you mean, you've lost it?
Plod I haven't got it any more, sir.
Drake What - you mean it's slipped into the lining of your jacket or something.
Plod I just turned my back for one minute to, you know, have a you-know-what, sir, and when I looked again, it was gone.
Drake Rolled away, had it?
Plod I don't know, sir.
Drake So, let me get this straight, Sergeant. I entrust you with the single most important piece of evidence we've yet uncovered - a dead man's head, no less, in a plastic bag - and you mislay it.
Plod Yes, sir.
Drake Never mind, Sergeant. These things happen, eh?
Plod Yes, sir. Thank you, sir. I knew you'd be okay about it.
Drake After all, we've only lost a head.
Plod Yes, sir.
Drake We'll just have to replace it, won't we?
Plod Arrgh!

Drake starts tugging at Plod's head, trying to pull it off.

Sabrina Inspector! What are you doing?
Drake Just pulling his head off. Don't worry, it won't in any way affect his abilities as a Policeman.
Sabrina You're killing him!
Drake That's right.
Sabrina Let him go!

Drake lets go. Plod shakes his head, then swiftly recovers.

Plod Oh, you've just jogged my memory, sir. I've got this for you. (*He hands over a file*)
Drake What is it?
Plod The file on Doctor Short. And I think you'll find it fascinating reading. For instance, did you know that Victoria Short was not Doctor Short's first wife, and that he'd been married three times before...
Drake (*joining in with Plod*)...not Doctor Short's first wife, and that he'd been

married three times before.

Plod You did know.

Drake Yes, Sergeant. But did you know that I was about to do this? (*He whacks him across the back of the head with the file*)

Plod No, sir.

Drake And what about this? (*This time Drake misses with his swipe, as Plod ducks*)

Plod Yes, I knew about that one, sir.

Drake stamps on his toe, by way of having the last word on the matter.

Sabrina Perhaps if you two spent less time squabbling you might get on with the important business in hand.

Drake What important business?

Sabrina Finding my step-mother!

Drake Ah, yes. The mother. Murderer? Or innocent victim? What do you think, Sergeant? Are we looking for a killer, or a killee?

Plod I've got a theory, sir.

Drake I can't wait. Fifty quid says it's a real corker.

Plod I think she was both.

Drake Both what?

Plod A killer and a victim.

Drake Mmm. Go on.

Plod Well, maybe she killed her husband by way of revenge.

Sabrina Revenge for what?

Plod For him murdering her.

Drake Yes. I think you may have a slight chronology problem there, Sergeant.

Plod A what, sir?

Drake Chronology, Sergeant, from the ancient Greek word "kronos".

Plod Kronos. What's that mean, sir?

Drake It means you're a thick turd, Sergeant. Leave the theories to me.

Plod Here, hang about. How would the ancient Greeks have known about me?

Sabrina Inspector, please! My mother.

Drake Don't worry, Miss Shortcake. I've got a sneaking suspicion that sooner or later, your mother will come walking through that door.

Enter Miss Short

Plod That's amazing!

A Flying Ducks Publication

Sabrina That's not my mother!
Miss Short Well of course I'm not your mother. Who are you?
Plod More to the point, Miss - who are we?
Drake Shut up, Sergeant.
Miss Short Where's Doctor Short?
Plod I'm afraid Doctor Short is tragically...

Drake silences Plod by sticking a banana in his mouth.

Drake Doctor Short is tragically...not well at the moment.
Miss Short Not well?
Drake A headache. A splitting headache.
Miss Short Sergeant, I demand to know who these people are and what they're doing here.

Plod responds according to the script below, but the banana in his mouth makes the sentence totally unintelligible.

Plod There's been an unfortunate crime committed here, miss. This is Inspector Drake of Scotland Yard - he's here to investigate.
Miss Short Inspector Drake. I'm sorry. I didn't realize.
Drake That's quite all right. Now, perhaps you'd like to tell us who are you?
Miss Short I'm Doctor Short's daughter - Sabrina!

There's a short, dramatic music stab, as Drake and Miss Short stare into a tight spotlight. The lights come back up.

Sabrina Don't believe her! She's lying!
Miss Short And who are you?
Sabrina I'm Doctor Short's daughter - Sabrina.

Another music stab, as this time Drake, Miss Short and Sabrina stare into the spotlight.

Plod In that case, they're both Doctor Short's daughter, Sabrina!

Plod lunges forward to stare into the spotlight - but this time there's no spotlight and no music. The others peel away.

A Flying Ducks Publication

Drake Not necessarily! One of them, is telling porkies!
Miss Short What on earth are porkies?
Plod Cockney rhyming slang, Miss. Porky pigs - lies!
Drake Shut up, Sergeant. Right - which one of you two is the real Sabrina Short?
Sabrina/Miss Short *(in unison)* I am!
Drake And which of you is the fake Sabrina Short?
Sabrina/Miss Short *(in unison)* She is!
Drake Right, that's sorted that out.
Miss Short Look, there's an easy way to settle this.
Drake Which is?
Miss Short Get my father in here. He'll verify who I am.
Drake I'm afraid that's not going to be possible.
Sabrina And she knows it! She's probably the one who killed him.
Miss Short Killed him? You mean he's...
Drake/Plod/Sabrina *(in unison)* Yes. As a dodo!
Drake And no-one leaves this house until I find out who murdered him.

Enter Doctor Short.

Short Who murdered who?
Miss Short Father!
Short Sabrina!

Plod faints. A spotlight narrows on Drake.

Drake Well bugger me.

Music. Curtain. End of Act One.

A Flying Ducks Publication

ACT TWO

Act Two starts with a re-enactment of the final moments of Act One. Well, almost. As the lights suddenly come up, the actors are caught slightly off-guard, chatting to each other. They quickly spring into position, and launch into the re-enactment as follows:

Miss Short Look, there's an easy way to settle this.
Drake Which is?
Miss Short Get my father in here. He'll verify who I am.
Drake I'm afraid that's not going to be possible.
Sabrina And she knows it! She's probably the one who killed him.
Miss Short Killed him? You mean he's...
Drake/Plod/Sabrina *(in unison)* Yes. As a penguin! *(Sheepishly)* Er...dodo.
Drake And no-one leaves this house until I find out who murdered him.

Enter Doctor Short.

Short Who murdered who?
Miss Short Father!
Short Sabrina!

Plod doesn't faint.

Drake Faint, Sergeant.
Plod Sorry, sir?
Drake Faint!
Plod We've done that bit, sir.
Drake I know! It's a re-enactment.
Plod A what?
Drake Do it again!
Plod Why?

Drake, losing patience, quickly grabs Plod's truncheon and belts him unconscious. Then he delivers his final line.

Drake Well bugger me! *(On cue, the music that ended Act One plays and the* *curtains start to close. Drake intervenes)* No! Stop! Stop it! We're carrying on this time! (*The music grinds to a halt, and the curtains jerkily open again*) Bloody amateurs. Oh, I've lost it now.

Short Will someone please tell me who's been murdered.

Drake Ah! You have!

Short I have.

Drake The Sergeant found your head. Tell him, Sergeant.

Plod (*still lying on the floor*) I found your head, sir.

Drake Get up.

Short And where exactly is this head?

Plod I lost it.

Drake He lost it.

Short Oh, you lost it.

Drake But it was definitely his head, wasn't it, Sergeant?

Plod Oh, it was definitely his head, sir.

Short You disappoint me, Drake. The Sergeant assured me you were a genius. I see now that he meant in comparison to himself.

Drake Your insults do not bother me, Doctor Short, but I would advise you not to rile the Sergeant here. What he lacks in intelligence, he also lacks in compassion.

Miss Short Daddy, I demand to know what this woman's doing here.

Sabrina Don't daddy him, you imposter!

Miss Short How dare you...

A fight breaks out between the two Sabrinas.

Drake Shut up! (*Drake and Plod dive in and separate the two women*) You - over there. You - over there. Sergeant - over here. (*He takes Plod to the front corner of the stage. Short is standing in the way*) And you - over there! (*He sends Short to the opposite corner*) Sergeant.

Plod Yes, sir?

Drake I'm confused.

Plod Yes, sir.

Drake The dead doctor is alive.

Plod Yes, sir.

Drake The missing wife is still missing.

Plod Yes, sir.

Drake And now we have two daughters.

Plod I've got a theory, sir.

Drake Don't even think about it, Sergeant.
Plod Right, sir.
Drake Erase the theory from your mind.
Plod I've already done so, sir.
Drake There's an old Hebrew saying, Sergeant. "Shakhram. Halakhram. Shakhram".
Plod What does it mean, sir?
Drake I don't know. But I intend to find out. You! (*He points to Miss Short*)
Miss Short Don't snap at me. I'm not a dog.
Drake I'll be the judge of that.
Miss Short Who the hell do you think you're talking to?
Drake I don't know - you tell me.
Miss Short I've already told you. My name is Sabrina Short.
Drake We already have one Sabrina Short, we don't need any more.
Miss Short She's an imposter.
Sabrina She's the imposter!
Miss Short Here!
Drake What's this?
Miss Short My passport. Perhaps you'd like to show us your passport, Miss whatever your name is.
Drake Well?
Sabrina I...er...I haven't got one.
Plod But you've just come back from Canada.
Sabrina I lost it. My handbag was stolen this morning.
Miss Short Well, well. How convenient.
Drake This looks genuine.
Miss Short That's because it is genuine.
Drake Sergeant.
Plod Sir?
Drake Over here. (*Drake struts to the opposite corner, quickly followed by Plod. Short is again in the way. Drake moves him on with an impatient flick of the head*) Now I'm really confused.
Plod Yes, sir.
Drake This woman would appear to be the real Sabrina Short.
Plod Yes, sir.
Drake But she can't be.
Plod No, sir.
Drake Why can't she be?
Plod I don't know, sir.

Drake Because Doctor Short has already identified the first Sabrina Short.
Plod Yes, sir.
Drake But now he's identified the second Sabrina Short.
Plod Yes, sir.
Drake And the first Sabrina Short is lying about her handbag.
Plod Yes, sir.
Drake Why?
Plod I don't know, sir.
Drake That's what we need to find out.
Plod Yes, sir.
Drake How long have you had this gift for conversation, Sergeant?
Plod I don't know, sir.
Drake I think you'd better leave the talking to me.
Plod Yes, sir.
Drake And don't say "yes, sir" again.
Plod No, sir.
Drake Or "no, sir".
Plod (*hesitant*) Righto.
Drake Righto, sir.
Plod Yes, sir.
Drake (*Drake slaps him on the nose with the passport, and then struts towards Sabrina*) You! What colour is your handbag?
Sabrina (*panicking*) Er..orange. Green. Purple. Brown.
Drake Orange, green, purple and brown, eh?
Sabrina Yes, it's a rather unusual one. A brown handle, with orange and green stripes, and purple spots.
Plod 'Er indoors has got one just like it, sir.
Miss Short Look, is someone going to tell me what the hell is going on, or have I got to call the Police?
Plod (*confidentially, to Drake*) Perhaps we'd better do as she says, sir. We don't want the Police mixed up in all of this.
Drake We are the Police.
Plod Good point, sir.
Short Drake, I'm holding you personally responsible for this mess.
Drake I've got just two questions for you, Doctor Short. First of all, why don't you tell us which of these two women is your real daughter? And secondly, and perhaps more importantly, why have you got a lamppost in your lounge?
Short I'm afraid I can't tell you anything, Inspector.
Drake Oh, you can't tell us. It's a quiz, is it?

A Flying Ducks Publication

Short If you had even half enough brains to solve this case, Drake, which I doubt, you'd know what the hell was going on here, and why I can't tell you. So why don't you just take this ridiculous two-man circus out of my house and leave us alone.

Drake Now you just listen to me, Doctor Shortarse. I've been willing to play this one by the book until now. But if you don't start cooperating *(pronounced with just four syllables, as before)* with me, and pretty damn quick, I'll have no alternative but to tell the Sergeant here to belt the living shite out of you!

Short All right, Drake. There's no point continuing this charade. Read this.

He produces a note. Plod snatches it from his hand, and reads it.

Plod Oh my good Gawd! *(Drake, over Plod's shoulder, turns the note the right way up)* Oh, my good Gawd!!*

Drake snatches the note, and reads it silently.

Drake *(under his breath)* Oh my good Gawd.

Short Now can you see why I didn't want to tell you!

Drake walks along the line of assembled bodies, who wait in suspense, like participants in an identity parade. He stops at Miss Short.

Drake Sergeant.

Plod Sir?

Drake Lock her up! *(He points behind him to Sabrina)*

Sabrina No!

There's a short burst of dramatic music, and the lights fade as Plod drags the screaming Sabrina away. As the music ends, the spotlight illuminates Plod under the lamppost.

Plod Well, I hope you amateur sleuths out there are following the story so far. Because this is where is starts to get complicated.

The spotlight fades on Plod. We hear the sound of a melancholy flute. The lights come up to reveal Drake, apparently playing the tune on his violin. Plod wanders over to him.

A Flying Ducks Publication

Plod Locked her in one of the bedrooms, sir.
Drake Good.
Plod Did you want me to strap her to the bed, sir?
Drake It's all right, Sergeant, I'll see to it later.
Plod Turning out to be a bit of a puzzler, eh, sir?
Drake Yes, it seems our friend the doctor is not quite as dead as you first thought.
Plod No, sir.
Drake Any theories, Sergeant?
Plod Only the obvious one, sir.
Drake The obvious one?
Plod Well, he's a doctor, isn't he?
Drake Yes.
Plod Well, there you go, then.
Drake There I go what?
Plod Well, he must have stitched his own head back on.
Drake Let me make a note of that one, Sergeant - that's a goodie. *(Pinching Plod's notebook and pencil)* "Stitched...own...head...back...on". You'll notice, Sergeant, that I haven't put it *right* to the top of my list.
Plod And forgive my presumption, sir, but in the circumstances it's the only explanation.
Drake The only explanation.
Plod Yes, sir.
Drake Let me try an alternative theory on you, Sergeant. Supposing, instead of the doctor having stitched his own head back on - a feat which, I think you'll agree, would have been a little tricky, even for a skilled surgeon at the top of his form, let alone a man who, at least until the latter stages of the operation, would not have had the use of his own head - instead of that, what if...and I know this is going to sound really wacky to you, Sergeant, but bear with me...what if...you were mistaken.
Plod No, sir.
Drake No, you're right. I must have been mad to doubt you. The stitched head theory's got to be the safe bet here, hasn't it. I mean, that's where all the smart money's going, isn't it, Sergeant. Stitched head, 2:1 favourite. Sergeant Plod wrong, 100:1 outsider.
Plod Do I detect a hint of irony in your remarks, sir?
Drake No, Sergeant, you do not detect a hint of irony in my remarks. What you detect in my remarks is the extremes of piss-taking. The head you saw...was not the doctor's.
Plod Oh, it was his all right. I'd recognise that mug anywhere.

A Flying Ducks Publication

Drake Sergeant, you've already admitted it was very dark down that cellar.
Plod I had my torch, sir.

Plod produces his torch. Drake snatches it from him. For later plot reasons, Drake should slip it into his trouser pocket.

Drake And that this man's head was cut into four pieces.
Plod I'm good at jig-saws.
Drake Nevertheless, hardly the ideal conditions for a positive identification, wouldn't you agree?
Plod *(smugly)* It was him all right.
Drake *(blowing his top)* Sergeant! It was not him!
Plod Oh, it was.
Drake It was not! People do not walk around once their head has been cut off! Would you like me to demonstrate?
Plod No, sir.
Drake Get out, Sergeant. I need to think. Go on, get out!

Plod exits, with sulky lip. Drake continues playing his violin, which this time emanates as a different instrument. Miss Short enters, unseen by Drake, and claps as he finishes the tune.

Miss Short That was beautiful.
Drake Thank you.
Miss Short I like a man who's master of his instrument.
Drake It's just something I like to pluck on.
Miss Short I remember when I was just 5 years old - we were on holiday in Italy - my father took me to see the great Paganini.
Drake Ah, yes. The escapologist.
Miss Short Well that night he was playing the violin. I was spellbound. I made my mind up there and then that I, Sabrina Short, would be one of the greatest virtuosos that ever lived. The next day, my father took me to a little music shop in the Piazza del Cina in the square and, well, our dreams never quite work out how we would like, do they Inspector.
Drake What happened?
Miss Short Oh, I don't know. My father's Italian wasn't too good. There was some confusion with the phrase book, and, well, let's just say, I play a mean bagpipe. Inspector, I've been very patient so far. Please, can you tell me what's going on here?

Drake Read this. (*He hands her the note*)

Miss Short Oh my good Gawd! (*Reading the note aloud*) "I'm coming to the house tonight. As far as the Police are concerned, I'll be your daughter from Canada. One slip up, and your wife is dead". What the hell's she up to?

Drake I don't know, yet. One thing's for sure, she didn't figure on the real Sabrina arriving back on the same night.

Miss Short Where is she now?

Drake Locked in a bedroom.

Miss Short Oh, Inspector, I'm scared.

Drake Don't be.

Miss Short Inspector?

Drake Mmm?

Miss Short Can I call you by your first name?

Drake No.

Miss Short Why not?

Drake Because you don't know what it is.

Miss Short Then why don't you tell me.

Drake Very well. It's...Indiana.

Miss Short Indiana. That's a fabulous name.

Drake It was my parents' idea.

Miss Short Indy.

Drake Yessy?

Miss Short Do you have a girlfriend, or a wife or anything?

Drake Not one that need concern us.

Miss Short In that case, would you think it terribly forward of me if I said that, every time I think of you, my nipples go as hard as wheel nuts?

Drake Well, maybe just a whisker forward, yes.

Miss Short I can't help it. You bring out the animal in me.

Drake Well, let's take the animal off its leash, shall we?

Miss Short Oh, Inspector, hold me! (*Her eyes light up as she presses against him*) Why, Inspector, I'm impressed! Is that for me?

Drake You'd better believe it, doll.

Miss Short Oh, Drake! Kiss me!

They go to kiss. Plod enters, on cue.

Plod Excuse me, sir.

Drake (*gritted teeth*) Yes, Sergeant.

Plod Thought I'd take a look outside, sir.

A Flying Ducks Publication

Drake Good. Toddle off, Sergeant.
Plod Only I wondered if you'd finished with my torch yet.

Drake angrily takes him to one side, and privately hands him the torch which was so effectively enhancing his reputation in his trouser pocket.

Drake Make it a good long look outside, Sergeant.
Plod Right, sir. G'night, Miss.
Miss Short Goodnight, Sergeant.

Plod exits through the french windows, with an embarrassing wink to Drake. Drake switches off the lights. We hear the rest of the dialogue from the darkness.

Drake Now, where were we?

He hugs her again.

Miss Short Why, Inspector? Gone off me already?
Drake Interruptions.
Miss Short Never mind. It shouldn't take me long to get you back in the mood. Kiss me!

A shaft of light from Plod's torch spotlights Drake and Miss Short as they are about to kiss.

Plod (*in a loud stage whisper*) Sir!
Drake (*a muted, frustrated whimper*) Mmmm?
Plod There's somebody outside, sir. He's up to no good.
Drake Lucky him.

Plod now uses his torchbeam to spotlight his own face - then that of Drake and Miss Short in turn, as each speaks.

Plod I'm sure I saw a shadowy suspect shambling through the shrubbery.
Drake Sho?
Plod It could be our murderer, sir!
Miss Short (*forced in speaking by receiving the spotlight of the torchbeam*) Er...he could be right, Inspector.
Drake All right, all right. I'll meet you out there, Sergeant.

A Flying Ducks Publication

Plod   Right, sir.

Plod exits through the french windows.

Drake   (*mumbling to himself*)   Be careful, Sergeant.   It's dark out there.   (*He switches on the light.   He is holding a revolver*)   I'd hate someone to accidentally shoot you.
Miss Short   I'll be waiting in my room, Inspector...if you need me, for anything.   Anything at all.

As she speaks, Miss Short is suggestively fondling the revolver that Drake is holding.   With a sudden squirt, we realize that it's a rather over-excited water pistol.   A disappointed Miss Short exits, wiping her face.   Drake is distraught, and in a sudden release of angry passion, he kicks Miss Short's suitcase, breaking his toe in the process.   There's an ominous tinkling sound of broken glass.   Drake, recovered, picks up the case, and tentatively opens it.   He pulls out a broken vase, and curses.   But then, delving deeper, he sees something which shocks him.

Drake   Oh my God!   What have I done?

Sabrina, also with a gun, creeps in through the french windows.

Sabrina   Freeze!   Drop the gun.   Over by the wall.
Drake   Not very original dialogue, Sabrina.
Sabrina   Shut up.   Just do it.
Drake   I can't freeze and drop the gun.
Sabrina   All right.   Freeze first, then drop the gun.
Drake   When you say, drop the gun...over by the wall, do you mean drop the gun over by the wall, or drop the gun here, and then move over to the wall over there.
Sabrina   That one.
Drake   Which one?
Sabrina   The second one.
Drake   Freeze first, then drop the gun here, then move over to the wall over there.
Sabrina   Yes.   Please.
Drake   How did you get out?
Sabrina   Through the window, and down the drainpipe.   (*Drake walks into the wall with a thud*).   Okay, that's far enough.   I'm sorry I have to do this, Drake. But it's the only way I can get you to listen to me.

A Flying Ducks Publication

Plod, unseen by all but the audience, walks past the french windows, and sees to his horror that Sabrina is holding Drake at gunpoint. He tiptoes out of sight.

Drake I'm listening.
Sabrina I'm innocent.
Drake I know.
Sabrina I'm Doctor Short's real daughter.
Drake I know.
Sabrina Well I don't give a damn what you...what did you say?
Drake I know. Look...

He reaches inside the suitcase. Sabrina twitches with the gun.

Sabrina Steady!
Drake Recognize this?

He pulls out Sabrina's multi-coloured handbag, which is exactly as described.

Sabrina My handbag!
Drake In the other Sabrina's suitcase. She stole it. And with it, your identity.
Sabrina But why? What's going on?
Drake I wish I knew. This plot has more twists in it than...a really twisted thing.
Sabrina I just wish I knew why my father was behaving so coldly towards me. He's just not himself tonight.
Drake What did you say?
Sabrina I said I wish I knew why...
Drake No, just the last bit!
Short Tonight.
Drake The bit before that.
Sabrina Oh, erm...he's just not himself.
Drake That's it!
Sabrina What?
Drake He's not himself. That's because he's someone else.
Sabrina You've lost me.
Drake The man upstairs is not your father.
Sabrina Don't be silly - of course he's my father.
Drake We already have two Sabrinas. What if we also have two Doctors? One real, one fake.
Sabrina But if that's not my father, then who....oh my God. Evil uncle Ebenezer?

Drake You have an evil uncle Ebenezer?

Sabrina My father's identical twin brother.

Drake Your father has an identical twin brother??

Sabrina The black sheep of the family.

Drake You have a black sheep in your family?

Sabrina When grandfather died, he left evil uncle Ebenezer without a penny. He was very jealous of my father.

Drake Your father has an identical twin brother who's a black sheep and who's very jealous of him and hasn't got a penny???

Sabrina Yes. Do you think there could be something in it?

Drake It's a vague possibility.

Sabrina There's just one thing wrong with your theory, Drake.

Drake There's nothing wrong with my theory. It's perfect.

Sabrina Uncle Ebenezer is dead.

Drake Okay, that's a setback.

Sabrina He and his girlfriend died last year in a boating accident. It was in all the papers. They went out in a little rowing boat - it capsized - their bodies were never fuh....! (*She stops mid-word in horror*)

Drake Their bodies were never fuh?

Short Found...oh, my God, Drake - you don't think?

Drake I'm afraid I do think. Tell me, was your uncle a member of the 200 Club?

Sabrina Yes, they both were. The only two brothers ever to qualify.

Drake Official Mensa records say there are now three members. Dr Short claims there are four. Who's the only person who wouldn't recognize the death of the fourth member?

Sabrina The fourth member!

Drake Precisely!

Sabrina Does this mean my father's...

Drake I'm afraid so.

Sabrina And my mother?

Drake I don't know. Good detectives never jump to conclusions. And neither do I. One thing's for sure. If your mother's alive, I'll find her - dead or alive.

Sabrina Oh, Drake. I'm scared.

Drake Don't be.

Sabrina Kiss me!

They move in to kiss. Plod lunges in through the door, and whacks Sabrina with the truncheon, felling her instantly.

A Flying Ducks Publication

Plod Gotcha!
Drake Well done, Sergeant.
Plod Thank you, sir.
Drake (*casually*) Have you got a priest or anyone you'd like to contact?
Plod Sir?
Drake Before I kill you.
Plod I'm not with you, sir.
Drake Oh, how I wish it could be so, Sergeant. This woman - the woman you
have just rendered unconscious - is the real Sabrina Short.
Plod (*disbelieving*) Naw!
Drake Yes! I'll kill you later, Sergeant. Right now you can help me get her on
the settee.
Plod Right, sir.

They struggle to lift Sabrina onto the settee. Drake starts gently tapping her face
to revive her.

Drake Sabrina. Sabrina. Sabby. Sab.

Plod speeds up the process by squirting her in the face with a soda syphon.
Sabrina comes back to life with a scream.

Drake It's all right. That's Sergeant Plod. Believe it or not he's on our side.
Sabrina, listen carefully. Do you feel strong enough to help me?
Sabrina I think so. What do you want me to do?
Drake Straighten me up. My back's gone.

Drake is bending over her, unable to move. Sabrina now jumps up, and helps Plod
to straighten up Drake.

Drake All right, Sergeant, now pay attention. I've solved the mystery of the head.
Not only do we have two Sabrinas, we also have two doctors. One dead, and
one alive.
Plod You mean...
Drake Precisely! A pair of Shorts.
Plod But how can that be, sir?
Sabrina You've heard of twin brothers haven't you, Sergeant?
Plod Why, yes, Miss! As a matter of fact, my brother had one.
Sabrina Did he, now?

A Flying Ducks Publication

Plod   As a matter of fact, he looked quite a lot like me.
Drake   But did he have your brains, Sergeant?
Plod   Yes, sir, I think he did.
Drake   Yes, I knew someone must have them. Sabrina - we must try to prove that the man upstairs is Ebenezer Short.
Sabrina   That's not going to be easy. They were identical in every way - mentally and physically - except...
Drake   Except what?
Sabrina   There was a difference, my father said, but...
Drake   But what?
Sabrina   Well, it's so tiny.
Drake   What is?
Sabrina   The mole. Uncle Ebenezer had a microscopic mole, apparently, on his...well, on his bottom. My father didn't. That's the only difference between them.
Plod   There is one other difference, Miss.
Sabrina   What?
Plod   Your father's got no head.
Drake   Shut up, Sergeant!
Plod   Right, sir.
Drake   We must get a look at that bottom.
Plod   Hang on a minute, I've got it!
Drake   What?
Plod   That bloke upstairs isn't Doctor Short at all. It's his twin brother!
Drake   Well done, Sergeant! I knew you hadn't lost the old sparkle.
Plod   But in that case, sir - who was the other geezer? The one who looked just like him?
Drake   I think we've done enough mental exercise for one day, haven't we, Sergeant.
Plod   Yes, sir.
Drake   Right. Down to work. Let's split up. One of us needs to get over to the library and get a copy of a local newspaper dated...what was the date of the boating accident?
Sabrina   Er...April. April the first.
Drake   April the first last year.
Plod   And the other one, sir?
Drake   (*putting his arm around him*) The other one, Sergeant, is on bottom duty. (*They stare each other out for a few seconds, then both dash for the door, wrestling to get out first*) All right, Sergeant. All right. We'll do this

A Flying Ducks Publication

democratically. Eeny, meany, miny, mo, catch a murderer by his toe. If he squeals, lets him go, eeny, meany, miny...mo. (*Drake, having started the rhyme pointing at Plod, is now pointing at himself. Plod has a smug look*) Damn. Well, that's me eliminated. You're on bottom duty, Sergeant. See you later.

Sabrina Wait! There's an old newspaper here, Inspector. It's a long shot, but...(*Sabrina grabs a newspaper from the waste-paper basket and blows off the dust*) Bingo! April the first!

Drake Right. Let's see if we're in luck.

Drake holds up the newspaper. The headline reads "Evil Uncle In Boat Tragedy".

Sabrina There, Drake! On the front!

Drake Aha! Blah, blah, blah...pictured here just before the tragedy are evil uncle Ebenezer, and in the background his girlfriend, Sophie Sausagedog. Sophie Sausagedog - S.S.

Sabrina Sabrina Short!

Plod Cybil Shepherd!

Drake I wonder. (*He looks at the picture with his magnifying glass*) Damn, it's too small. Sergeant. This photograph. The bit in the background, there, with the girlfriend. I want you get it blown up.

Plod Right, sir.

Plod exits with the paper.

Drake Oh, no. What have I said?

There's a large explosion.

Drake (*shouting through the door*) Sergeant? Are you all right?

Plod (*casually and cheerfully*) No, sir.

Drake What happened?

Plod I appear to have blown myself up, sir.

Drake Badly?

Plod Oh, quite badly, yes sir.

Drake I think you'd better get back in here.

A blackened Plod enters. His hat is split like a banana skin and smoking.

Drake You know, Sergeant, sometimes you're so predictable.

A Flying Ducks Publication

Plod In what way, sir?
Drake Sergeant. Get over to the local library. Get another copy of the newspaper. Take it to the lab, And have the picture...enlarged.
Plod And then I blow it up, sir.
Drake No, and then you bring it back here to me. Got it?
Plod Yes, sir.
Drake Sure?
Plod Almost positive, sir.
Drake Good. Because if you get it wrong this time, I shall have no alternative but to kick your spine right through the top of your head. Do I make myself clear, Sergeant?
Plod Sounds fair to me, sir.
Drake Good. Toddle off. Oh, and Sergeant - while you're out (*he reaches for a piece of the broken vase*) see if you can get another vase like this one.
Plod You mean broken, sir?
Drake Never mind.

Plod exits. Short enters, wearing a dressing gown, with no pyjamas.

Short What the hell was that noise?
Drake Ah, Doctor Short and Curlies. What's the matter - couldn't sleep?
Short I heard an explosion.
Drake Explosion? Did you hear an explosion?
Sabrina No.
Drake It was probably your conscience keeping you awake.
Short Why isn't this woman in prison?
Drake She's still helping me with my enquiries.
Short (*leaning over the chessboard*) Well, I trust you know what you're doing, Inspector.
Drake Oh, don't worry, we're making progress.
Short Really? (*With a wry smile, he makes his chess move*) Rook takes bishop. Goodnight, Inspector.
Drake Oh, by the way. Your wife rang.

Short, almost by the door, stops in his tracks, and for a split second looks shocked.

Short That's impossible!
Drake Oh? (*Making his move*) Why? Check.
Short (*he composes himself and turns*) Because I think you'll find that your

Sergeant has cut the phone line. (*He makes his move*)
Drake (*coolly*) A lucky escape.
Short Luck doesn't come into it, Inspector.

Again he is almost at the door when Drake stops him.

Drake One last question. (*He makes a move*) I understand this is your fourth wife.
Short That's not a question. It's a statement.
Drake I understand this is your fourth wife, do I? Pass me the file.

Sabrina passes him a nail file. Drake quickly files a nail.

Drake Now pass me that wallet thing with papers in. (*She does, and Drake begins to study it*) Your first wife died of a heart attack.
Short That's right.
Drake She was eighteen years old, and a member of the Tipton Harriers.
Short It could happen to anyone.
Drake Your second wife was athletic too, wasn't she, doctor. A swimmer.
Short That's right.
Drake Butterfly and breaststroke. British champion. Commonwealth champion. Olympic silver medallist. Bronze in the relay.
Short You've done your homework, Inspector.
Drake So, can you explain how she came to drown in the bath?
Short I believe she banged her head on the tap. The coroner went through all this at the time.
Drake And Mrs Short number three. The one who, while out walking the dog, was squashed by a runaway garden roller...
Short Terrible business. The grave takes up more than half an acre.
Drake All in all, you haven't had a lot of luck with women, have you?
Short Not yet. I assume there's a point to dragging all this up, is there, Inspector? These memories are very painful to me.
Drake Not half as painful as they were to your ex-wives.
Short Why don't you just tell me exactly what's going on in your mind, Inspector. I'm sure it can't be very much.
Drake Nobody likes a sarcastic mass murderer.
Short Ah, at last! The great Inspector has finally had the courage to make an attacking move. All right. Let's suppose for one moment that you're right, Drake. Let's suppose I did murder my wife. Let's suppose that every drop of

blood has been meticulously scrubbed from the scene of the crime. That the murder weapon has been dissolved in acid. That the clothes I was wearing were burned in that very hearth. Where's your evidence, Drake? Where's your motive? Where's your proof? No. The simple fact is, you've been outwitted every step of the way, and you can't touch me, Drake. You simply can't touch me! Ugggh! Bloody hell!

Plod, who entered towards the end of Short's speech, decides that he can touch Short, with a truncheon, and does so. Short crashes to the floor.

Drake Sergeant, you really shouldn't do things like that.
Plod No, sir.
Drake Still, what's done's done, eh, Sergeant?
Plod Yes, sir.
Drake Can't be helped.
Plod Would you like me to dissolve the truncheon in acid, sir?
Drake Later, Sergeant. Right now, we've got a microscopic mole to find. Come on.

They struggle to get him draped over the settee, facing the audience.

Sabrina He practically owned up to it! He's playing games with you, Inspector.
Drake Don't worry. Whatever he's up to, we'll soon get to the bottom of it. Right. (*He lifts up Short's dressing gown*) Stand back, Sabrina. This is man's work. In you go, Sergeant.
Plod But sir...
Drake Do it!

Plod disappears underneath Short's dressing gown. There's much murmuring and deliberating before he finally re-appears.

Drake Well?
Plod Hard to say, sir.
Drake Why?
Plod He's wearing boxer shorts.
Drake Then take them off, Sergeant.
Plod But...
Drake Now!

Plod again disappears under the raised dressing gown. After some grunting and movement, he emerges with the shorts draped over the end of his truncheon. He tentatively drops them in the waste-paper basket, and wipes the end of his truncheon on his tunic.

Drake   Quickly Sergeant. Before he comes round.

Plod again disappears.

Plod   How big's microscopic, sir?
Drake   Not very. Well?
Plod   Nothing, sir.
Drake   Are you sure?
Plod   Positive.
Drake   Whereabouts on his bottom was this mole?
Sabrina   I don't know!
Drake   Search everywhere, Sergeant.
Plod   I have, sir.
Drake   Search...every nook and cranny.
Plod   But, sir...
Drake   That's an order, Sergeant.
Plod   Sir. (*Plod takes out his torch, switches it on, disappears again for a few seconds, and pops back up)* Every nook?
Drake   And cranny, Sergeant.
Plod   (*from underneath the dressing gown)* What exactly does a mole look like, sir?
Drake   Well, it's sort of a...brown...thingy.
Plod   (*emerging*) Nothing, sir.

Drake   There must be!
Plod   No, sir. Every nook. Every cranny. No brown thingies.
Drake   Damn!
Sabrina   Perhaps we're wrong. Perhaps it is my father after all.
Drake   No. He's clever. He's damn clever. He's probably covered the mole with make-up. Check it out, Sergeant.
Plod   How the f...
Drake   I don't know! Just...wet your finger, and rub it around a bit.

Plod tears the stripes from his jacket, hands them to Drake, and heads for the

A Flying Ducks Publication

door.

Drake What are you doing, Sergeant?
Plod Resigning, sir.
Drake All right, all right. I'll do it. Come here. Hold this up.
Sabrina Hurry up. He's coming round!

Plod grabs the dressing gown, as Drake rolls up his one sleeve.

Drake Right, lend me your finger, Sergeant.

Drake grabs Plod's finger, sucks it, and thrusts it under the dressing gown.
Short's face registers shock, then his eyebrows raise, and he smiles inanely. Miss
Short enters.

Miss Short What the hell are you doing?
Drake Just a routine enquiry.
Miss Short I've heard about people like you!
Plod If he's going to prison he'd better start getting used to this.
Miss Short Are you all right, father?
Short Not now, Sabrina!
Miss Short Inspector Drake - I'm going to report you to your superiors.
Drake (*angrily*) Inspector Drake has no superiors, Miss Shitehawk. Or should
   I call you...Sophie Sausagedog?
Miss Short I don't know what you mean. Sophie Sausagedog was my uncle's
   girlfriend. And she's dead.
Drake Is she? Is she, now. Sergeant - did you get the photograph?
Plod Yes, sir, but...
Drake Fetch it.

Plod fetches a large photograph from just outside the door. The audience only
sees the back.

Drake The game's up, Sophie. This photograph conclusively proves that you are
   not Sabrina Short, daughter of Doctor Short, but in fact...(*he looks at the*
   photograph)...shit!
Miss Short You were saying?
Drake That will be all for now, Sabrina.
Short Have you finished with me, too, Inspector?

A Flying Ducks Publication

Drake For the time being.
Short You disappoint me, Inspector. I was hoping I could play my little game against a more worthy opponent. Black Knight takes White queen. Let me know when you're ready to concede defeat.. Goodnight.

Short exits, like a saddle-sore cowboy. Miss Short follows, stopping on the way out to retrieve his boxer shorts from the waste-paper basket.

Miss Short No-one treats the Shorts like this.

She exits.

Drake Damn!
Plod (*taking the photograph*) You were hoping that this would be her.
Drake Yes.
Plod But it isn't.
Drake No.
Plod So, what's our next move, sir?
Drake We have to find that mole. It's our only hope.
Sabrina (*producing another newspaper - this time from the bookshelves*) I think this might interest you, Drake.
Drake What is it?
Sabrina Take a look at the story on page four.
Drake Cor!
Sabrina Page four.
Drake Oh. (*He turns over one page*)
Sabrina There. Look at the headline.
Drake "National Health Outcry As Mystery Man Has Free Op To Remove Microscope Mole From Bottom". Damn! He's thought of everything. Now we'll never prove who he is.
Plod I could always try and beat a formal confession out of him, sir.
Drake You'd never manage it.
Plod No, sir. But I'd enjoy trying.
Sabrina He's beaten us.
Drake No.
Plod She's right, sir.
Drake No!! He's slipped up, somewhere. I know he has. But how? Where? When? Who? Whither? Whence? Why...am...I...talking...like...this?
Sabrina The poison!

Drake What?

Sabrina You said he tried to poison me, with the injection. And you can prove it! Surely that's enough to arrest him.

Drake He's thought of that too. Remember the note? He'd simply stick to his story that you were a blackmailing imposter threatening his wife. Who could blame him for trying to protect his family? He'd have the jury eating out of his hand. Oh, yes, he's a smart one all right.

Plod Well, g'night, sir.

Drake Where the hell do you think you're going?

Plod Home, sir. I told 'er indoors I'd only be ten minutes. That was three days ago.

Drake You're not going anywhere until I crack this case.

Sabrina Inspector, please. The Sergeant's right. You both need some rest.

Drake Rest? I can't rest, Sabrina. Not while I know there's a killer on the loose. Not while there are wrongs to be righted, and terrible injustices to be...justiced. I'll never rest, while I know there's a man up there who's putting up two evil, blood-stained fingers to the rest of society. Whose machiavellian greed preys on decent citizens like you, and me, and...and Bambi. No, Sabrina. No matter how long it takes. A week. A month. A year. I shall never rest, until your name is cleared, and that man is firmly behind bars.

Sabrina Oh, Drake! Kiss me!

They close into an embrace.

Plod Let's face it, sir. You're not going to crack this one.

Drake (*pulling away just before the kiss*) What did you say?

Plod You're good, sir. I mean, you're the best. But you've met your match this time. He's beaten us. It's the perfect crime.

Drake No!!! (*Grabbing Plod's throat*) There's no such thing as a perfect crime. I've never been beaten, Sergeant. Do you hear me? Never! And I'm not going to be beaten now.

Sabrina Drake! No! You're killing him! (*Drake breaks away, distressed*) You're just tired.

Drake No. The Sergeant's right. Deep down I knew, one day, this moment would come. It's time to hang up my hat.

Plod I'll do that for you, sir.

Drake (*snatching his hat back*) It's just an expression, Sergeant.

Sabrina But why?

Drake Why? Because I've been beaten.

A Flying Ducks Publication

Sabrina By a man with an IQ of over two hundred. That's nothing to be ashamed of.

Drake It's enough. For me, it's enough.

Sabrina But this is just one case. There's no need to give up your job.

Drake Job? Job? This isn't my job, Sabrina. This is my life. Goodbye. I'm sorry things couldn't have worked out better. (*Sabrina is in tears*) Goodbye, Sergeant. And thank you.

Plod What for, sir?

Drake For your loyalty.

Plod It's been a privilege, sir.

Drake moves slowly towards the door.

Sabrina Drake. Before you go. Do one last thing for me.

Drake If it's in my power.

Sabrina It is. Kiss me.

Drake sidles warily over to her. Plod stands motionless.

Drake Sergeant. Stand over there.

Plod Right, sir.

Drake Look the other way.

Plod Yes, sir.

Drake And don't say a word.

Plod No, sir.

Sabrina, standing behind the settee, puckers her lips. Drake folds her into his arms and leans her back. Inches from her lips, there's a dramatic drone of music. Drake has apparently spotted something behind the settee. His eyes widen, and he lets go of Sabrina, who yelps as she crashes down behind the settee.

Drake Oh my God! That's it.

Plod What is?

Drake It's been staring me in the face.

Plod What has?

Drake I've got him, Sergeant.. I've bloody got him!

Sabrina (*emerging, bedraggled, from behind the settee*) What have you found?

Drake I told you, Sergeant. I told you there was no such thing as a perfect crime. I knew he'd made a mistake. I've bloody got him!

A Flying Ducks Publication

Sabrina Inspector, please! Let us in on the secret!
Drake Later. Sergeant - I want you to assemble everyone in this room in precisely one hour. Have you got that?
Plod Where are you going, sir?
Drake One hour, Sergeant. It's time...for a showdown!

Dramatic music. Lights fade to a spotlight on Plod.

Plod Exciting, isn't it! Well, all we have to do now, is wait an ιour. (*There's a long pause. Plod whistles to pass the time, then checks his watch*) Twenty-four seconds. Oh, bugger this.

There's a harp glissando, and Plod 'wobbles', mimicking the film convention of the shimmering picture to represent the passage of time. The lights come up, to reveal Miss Short, anxiously pacing, Dr Short, sitting calmly, and Sabrina, also looking nervous. The harp glissando has stopped. Plod is still wobbling.

Sabrina It's been almost an hour, Sergeant.

Plod stops wobbling.

Plod Inspector Drake is never late, Miss.
Miss Short So, what exactly is this startling new evidence you've uncovered, Sergeant?
Plod Ah! (*Tapping his nose, smugly*) You'll have to wait and see, won't you, Miss.
Miss Short You don't know, do you.
Plod No, Miss.
Short Well, whatever it is, we won't have long to wait. Five seconds to go. Three, two, one...

There's a knock on the door. Plod opens it. Drake enters, wearing a silly Groucho-style plastic disguise kit - false nose, glasses, etc.

Plod Sorry, sir - you can't come in here. This is a murder investigation.
Miss Short Sergeant - that's Inspector Drake.
Plod What? (*Drake removes his disguise*) Good Lord above! That's uncanny, sir.
Short Inspector Drake. I must congratulate you.

A Flying Ducks Publication

Drake What for?

Short Oh, the theatrical entrance. I'm sure Agatha Christie would have been very proud of you. The protagonists all gathered, waiting anxiously for the surprise denouement.

Drake New what?

Short But listen carefully, Drake. This new "evidence" that you're about to present - this circumstantial, uncorroborated claptrap you've managed to dream up - it may be great fun for parlour games, but it will never stand up in a court of law.

Drake A court of law? Well, let's see, shall we? (*Drake turns to the audience*) Ladies and gentlemen of the jury. I want to tell you...a story. A story of man so consumed with jealousy for his own brother that he systematically murdered all his wives - because he couldn't stand to see him happy. But even that wasn't enough to satisfy this man's grotesque hatred. So he started to plan what he believed would be...the perfect crime. What better way to steal a man's house, his wealth, his self respect, than to become that man. So he fakes his own death, murders his twin brother, and takes his place. Then brutally murders the only woman who could tell them apart - his brother's last wife, Victoria.

Short Bravo! Excellent, Drake. You're a more worthy opponent than I gave you credit for. But it's like you said. A story. Your word against mine. What we have here, Inspector, is stalemate.

Drake Sit down, Doctor. I have another move to make. You see, this is a story with a twist. (*Producing the disguise*) Would you mind trying this on for me.

He puts the disguise on Miss Short.

Sabrina Hang on. I've seen her somewhere before.

Drake Yes, that's right. You have. In a local newspaper. (*He holds the blown up photograph next to her face. It shows a lady with the same disguise*)

Miss Short That's pathetic! It could be anyone under that disguise!

Drake Yes, you're right. It could be...anyone. (*He pops the disguise onto Sabrina*) Even you, Sabrina. Or should I call you...Sophie Sausagedog!

Sabrina Drake - what are you saying?

Drake Oh, you were good, Sophie. Very good. Planting your own handbag in the real Sabrina's suitcase to make it look as though she'd stolen it - that was a masterstroke. And I almost fell for it.

He again falls off the stage.

A Flying Ducks Publication

Miss Short Indiana? Are you all right?
Plod Indiana?
Drake Shut up, Sergeant.
Plod But your name's Cecil, sir.
Drake Pull me up! (*Plod tries to pull him up, but succeeds only in tearing off his other sleeve. Drake makes his way back onto stage via the steps*) The problem with greedy men, Sophie, is that they don't like sharing. Not even with their own girlfriend.
Sabrina (*her nerve finally cracks, and she turns on Short*) You tried to kill me with that syringe, you bastard!
Short Shut up! He's got nothing.
Drake Luckily, the poisoned syringe stuck in Sergeant Plod, where it could do no damage. And once you realized that he was out to get you, you told me just enough to ensure that he, and the real Sabrina, were locked away for good, leaving you to enjoy your massive inheritance. Very clever, Sophie.
Sabrina But not clever enough for the great Inspector Drake, eh?
Drake You should have shot me while you had the chance.
Sabrina Yes, well I never make the same mistake twice.

She pulls out a gun, and fires three shots directly at Drake.

Miss Short Drake! Duck!

Miss Short dives on him, and they disappear behind the settee. Three ducks falls off the wall to the ground. Drake jumps back up, and examines the wall where the ducks were.

Drake Congratulations, Sophie. You win a cuddly teddy. (*He grabs one from behind the settee and presents it to Sabrina*) Let's hope he likes porridge.
Plod (*he laughs heartily, but then instantly stops*) I don't get it, sir.
Drake Take her away, Sergeant!
Plod Right, sir! Come along with me, you!

Plod grabs Miss Short.

Drake No, Sergeant - that one!
Plod Oh, right, sir. Come along with me, you!
Miss Short (*emerging from behind the settee*) Are you all right?
Drake Thanks to you.

A Flying Ducks Publication

Plod (*at the doorway, handing Sabrina over to an imaginary Constable*) Take her away, Constable. (*With his hand over his mouth*) Right you are, sir.

Sabrina exits.

Short Bloody fool!
Drake Oh, don't be too hard on her, Doctor. After all, it wasn't her that made the fatal mistake. It was you.
Short Never.
Drake Oh, yes. You were careful to destroy the murder weapon. You burnt the blood-stained clothes in the hearth. You meticulously bleached the bloodstains from the settee. You even removed the microscopic mole from your own bottom. But you see Doctor, you forgot...to remove the body!

They look down behind the settee. There's a dramatic stab of music.

Short Oh, shit.
Drake (*knocking over the Black King*) Checkmate. Take him away, Sergeant!!

Plod takes Short out, murmuring as he goes.

Short Hundred.
Plod Two hundred.
Short One-fifty.
Plod Done.

Miss Short goes to look behind the settee, Drake tries to stop her.

Drake I wouldn't.

She still does, and screams hysterically. Drake can't stop her, and is about to raise his hand to slap her, when Miss Short suddenly slaps Drake's face hard, and stops screaming.

Miss Short I'm all right now.
Drake Don't cry.
Miss Short I'm sorry. First my marriage breaks up, then my mother disappears, then my father's head is chopped into four pieces, then a woman turns up claiming to be me, then my father comes back from the dead, then I'm arrested,

then I discover my father is dead after all, then my mother...it's just been a funny week.

Drake I know.

Miss Short One thing's for sure, Uncle Ebenezer is off my Christmas list. Oh, Drake - is it over now?

Drake It's over now. Murder, attempted murder, fraud - they'll be locked away for weeks.

Miss Short What a waste. Such a brilliant mind. I can't believe he made such an elementary mistake.

Drake He didn't.

Miss Short What?

Drake An old detectives trick. Your opponent doesn't have to make a mistake. You just have to make him think he has. This woman isn't your step-mother.

Miss Short It isn't?

Drake It's her identical twin sister, Griselda.

Miss Short No!

Drake (*apparently lifting up a skirt*) Yes. See the mole, there?

Miss Short Oh, yes.

Drake When I told her what had happened, fortunately, she agreed to take part in a little experiment to trap him. Unfortunately, to make it look realistic, I had to kill her, but that's showbizz.

Miss Short Drake, that's brilliant!

Drake Yes. Perfect. I've cracked the perfect crime. I've found the perfect woman. And, with Sergeant Plod half-way to the local nick, I've got rid of the perfect pillock!

Miss Short Oh, Drake! Take me!

Miss Short pulls a clip from her hair, letting it cascade onto her shoulders. Drake takes off his hat, and a wig of flowing hair cascades over his shoulders. Miss Short reclines onto the settee, and opens her arms for him. He places one hand on the settee, leaps over it, lands on the false middle cushion from which he first appeared, and disappears without trace. (See production notes for alternative ending) Music. Curtain.

A Flying Ducks Publication

NOTES

NOTES